Joseph Jeremiah O'Keefe

The Buildings and Churches of the Mission of Santa Barbara

Joseph Jeremiah O'Keefe

The Buildings and Churches of the Mission of Santa Barbara

ISBN/EAN: 9783337039134

Printed in Europe, USA, Canada, Australia, Japan

Cover: Foto ©Andreas Hilbeck / pixelio.de

More available books at **www.hansebooks.com**

THE BUILDINGS AND CHURCHES

—OF—

THE ✳ MISSION

—OF—

SANTA BARBARA.

A HANDBOOK

—OF—

AUTHENTIC INFORMATION ON THE MISSION OF SANTA BARBARA,
FROM ITS FOUNDATION TO THE PRESENT DAY.

Translated, written and compiled from the Register, reports, and other
documents in the Archives of the Mission.

BY REV. J. J. O'KEEFE, O. S. F.

Member of the Community at the Mission.

SANTA BARBARA, CAL.:
INDEPENDENT JOB PRINTING HOUSE.
1886.

INTRODUCTION.

Much has been written on California in general, and not a little on this county in particular, but very little, so far, that can be relied upon as authentic, has been written on the MISSION of Santa Barbara. Now, therefore, I shall endeavor in these few pages to give what *authentic* information I possess regarding the founding, buildings, the several churches erected, and various other facts connected with, and relating to this Mission, from its foundation to the present day.

JOSEPH J. O'KEEFE, O. S. F.

Santa Barbara Mission.

CHAPTER I.

The joy of the great Father Junipero Serra cannot be described, when he saw that everything was prepared at last, to establish the projected Missions of Santa Barbara Channel, an event for which his soul had yearned so long. Accordingly San Buenaventura, at the eastern extremity of the channel, was founded on March 31, 1782. A short time after, or about the middle of April, Governor Felipe de Neve, accompanied by Father Junipero Serra, set out with sixty soldiers and their respective officers, to establish the Presidio and Mission of Santa Barbara.

The party marched along the shore, observing with all attention, compatible with the distance, the islands that form the channel. Arriving at a place they considered about nine leagues from the Mis-

sion of San Buenaventura, a halt was ordered by
the Governor, who, in company with Father Junipero and a few soldiers, reconnoitered the neigh-
borhood with the object of selecting a good location
for the Presidio.   They found this on a large rancheria of many Indians, a short distance from the
shore, where it gracefully curves and forms a sort
of small bay, in which they judged good anchorage
would be found.   Orders were immediately given
to march, occupy this place and encamp.

The Governor immediately began to make a
large cross, build a booth for a temporary chapel,
and a table for an altar; having finished these, the
place was blessed by Father Junipero, the cross
raised, Mass celebrated, at which the Governor
and troops assisted, Father Junipero preached, and
the ceremony concluded by taking possession of
the place, without the slightest contradiction or
opposition of the natives.

Thus the PRESIDIO of Santa Barbara was founded on the 29th of April, 1782.

CHAPTER II.

The founding of the Mission, it seems, should
have followed immediately, and progressed simul-
taneously with the Presidio.   The venerable
Father Junipero, believing this would be the case,

consented to remain in the meantime, with the Governor at the Presidio, for the benefit of the soldiers and their families (for nearly all were married). Seeing the Governor remained silent on a matter of such importance, he finally urged him to lend assistance in founding the Mission. The Governor replied that he did not intend to consent to the founding of the Mission until he should have finished the Presidio. "Then your excellency," replied Father Junipero, "as there is nothing more for me to do here at present, I shall return to Monterey, and meet the vessels that are expected, but that so many people may not be without a priest, I shall call one from San Juan Capistrano;" which he did immediately, and then started for his Mission of San Carlos at Monterey, where he allowed himself a little rest, (all his journeys were invariably made on foot). Then he began his visitation to the other Missions, confirming in each, all the Indians who had been instructed and baptized. He continued to work up to the month of August, 1784, when he was completely prostrated, and immediately sent for Father Palou, who left San Francisco and arrived at San Carlos on the 18th of the same, remaining with Father Junipero until his death, which occurred a little before 2 o'clock p. m., on the 28th of August, 1784.

I do not intend to write the biography of the

venerable Junipero Serra, nor is it necessary, as, I understand, this has been ably done by Very Rev. Joachim Adan, Vicar General of this Diocese, but I judged it would be well, if not entirely necessary, to give the few incidents above recorded, in order to show the extent of his connection with, and relation to, the Channel Missions, (so called at that time,) more especially this of Santa Barbara, which he was on the point of actually founding, when delayed by the circumstances above related, and thereby deprived of the pleasure he so ardently desired.

CHAPTER III.

On the death of the venerable Father Junipero Serra, Father Palou, his intimate friend, companion and biographer, was chosen President of the Missions, although much against his will, because he intended to depart shortly for Mexico, to superintend the publication of the "life and virtues" of Father Junipero Serra, published in Mexico in 1787, and other works he had in print, but he could not depart until August, 1785. During his year of office his official acts were very few and of little or no importance, and *no mission* was founded during his term. I make this statement because Forbes, in his "California," page 80, mentions that Father Palou's first act on becoming President, was to found the Missions of Santa Barbara and La Purisima, a manifest error, (which has been copied by John Gilmary Shea, in his "History of the Catholic Missions, among the Indian Tribes of the United States,") as Father Palou was not in California, when these Missions were founded.

Yearly, on the fourth day of December, the Holy Catholic Church celebrates the feast of Santa Barbara, Virgin and Martyr. On this day A. D. 1786, the holy cross was raised, nearly one mile from the Presidio, on the Mission site, called in Spanish "el pedragoso," in the native tongue, "Taynayam," and from this day dates the founding of the Mission. Very Rev. Father Fermin Francisco de Lasuen, President of the Missions, on the 15th of the same month, in a hut or booth made for the occasion, with the boughs or branches of trees, on the above mentioned site, celebrated Mass and preached, at which the Governor (Pedro Fages) accompanied by a few soldiers, assisted.

Father President Lasuen, named as first Minister of this Mission, the Rev. Antonio Paterna, and as his associate, Rev. F. Christobal Oramas. No buildings could be erected during the remainder of this year, on account of the heavy and continued rain.

CHAPTER IV.

The work of building commenced in 1787. The first in order being a house for the Priests which was 16x5 varas, a kitchen 6x5 varas, then the first church or chapel 14x5 varas, a servant's room 6x5 varas, a granary 21x5, another house for the unmarried women, 12x5 varas. For brevity's sake, in giving the dimensions of all the buildings in the order of erection, I shall use the measurement of the vara, as above; this measure is a little less than our yard, or about 34 inches, universally used in Spain and Mexico, and still heard in California, particularly in real estate business. A carpenter's shop was erected, 10x5 varas, and served, ad interim, as a lodge for unmarried men, also four more rooms, respectively, two 6x6, 5x6, 8x6. Owing to the rain these could not be roofed in.

All the above named buildings, rooms, etc., were built of adobe walls one vara thick; the roofing was of heavy rafters, across which long poles or canes were tied, a layer of soft clay or mud was spread over these, then finished or thatched with straw. This style of roofing was simply provisional till they could begin manufacturing tiles.

The number of Indians existing at the end of this year, in the Mission is given at 183.

From January until the month of July, 1788, no farther progress was made in building, owing to the scarcity of provisions for the support of the

Indians; during that month a supply was received and work resumed. Tiles were now being manufactured and the work done from July till December 31st of this year was as follows, viz: The four rooms mentioned were finished with tile roof; also the apartments used by the women and girls. The apartments of the men were also tiled and used after for a granary; a new house was erected for them 12x5 varas, with tile roof. The Church was extended a little and roofed with tiles, the walls of the extension were ($\frac{1}{2}$) half vara thick.

Indians existing in the Mission at the end of July, 260; to end of December, 307.

CHAPTER V.

The second Church of this Mission was erected in 1789, adobe walls, dimensions 30x5 varas. The first, considered much too small, was taken down. A larger granary was also built 31x7; adjoining this was erected an apartment 12x7, to which the women were changed; also two rooms 5x4$\frac{1}{2}$, and one 9x5 for muleteers and their packs, the walls of all the above were adobe, well plastered and roofed with tiles.

Indians existing in the Mission on the last of December this year, 425.

The buildings erected in 1790 were, two houses

each 10x6 varas and divided into two rooms, for
the Priests' use; another house 60x6 varas, divided
into eight rooms, for dining room, kitchen, hall.
store room, fuel room, lockup, flour and meal room,
and a room for the women and girls; one 12x7
was built for a granary. All these were of adobe
walls, well plastered with mortar to better protect
them against the rain, and roof of tiles.

Number existing at the end of this year in
Mission, 407; plus from Presidio, 22.

A guard house was erected in 1791, 10x6; a
carpenter shop, and two other rooms, for housing
tools and agricultural implements.

Number of persons existing at the end of this
year, 499.

Two large corrals were made in 1792, with
stone walls, one for black cattle, the other for
sheep. The former 90x75 varas, the latter 75x50
varas.

Indians existing at Mission, 500.

The third Church of this Mission was commenced in 1793, of adobe, size 45x9¼, Sacristy 9¼x5
varas, a brick portico in front of Church, wall well
plastered with mortar and all roofed with tiles.

Number of Indians existing at the end of year,
541.

The large adobe Church, containing six chapels,
was finished in 1794. A granary 26x7 and a
weaving room 18x7 were built also.

The report of this year records the death of Rev. Fr. Antonio Paterna, the founder and first Minister of this Mission.

Indians existing at the end of this year, 549.

The principal branch of industry, is the carding and weaving of wool into blankets and cloth for the Indians. The crops of this year were a complete failure, the Ministers had to have recourse to the Missions of La Purisima and San Luis, whence they received wheat and corn.

During 1795 the roof of two sides and one-half of the square of this Mission was renovated. The old beams and rafters of sycamore and poplar, being completely rotten, were replaced by beams and rafters of pine; and four small rooms of stone, brick and mortar were added to the Priests' dwelling.

Indians existing in Mission at the end of this year, 569.

The remaining part of the square, was roofed anew in 1796. So all the buildings were renovated, beams and rafters of good pine having been used to replace the old of sycamore and poplar.

A corridor was built in front of the side facing the Presidio, roof of tiles and pillars of brick and mortar, dimensions 45x3 varas. This is a great protection to the walls, from the rain which beats in from the south and southeast. In the weavers' courtyard a corridor was also made, pillars of adobe, dimensions 18x3, two small rooms, one at each end, 6x3 varas.

Indians existing at end of this year, 646.

A new square and courtyard was marked in 1797, and three granaries built, each 25x6 varas, a room 6x6, another 10x6 for leather, and one of 9x6 for a blacksmith's forge, another of same size for general use or for fowls. All these are adobe walls, well plastered inside and outside with mortar. Although they form a distinct courtyard yet, there is an entrance to it, from the old one of the Mission.

Total of existing Indians at the Mission at the end of this year, 782.

CHAPTER VI.

As the Indians were now increasing rapidly, it became necessary to form a village, and give to each family a separate house; land was then set aside adjoining the Mission, and in 1798 nineteen houses were erected to contain that number of families; the rooms were 6½x4 varas, roofed with tile, plastered and whitewashed, both inside and out. Moreover a piece of land was inclosed by a wall 1200 varas long by 3 varas high, to be cultivated as a kitchen garden, vineyard and orchard, the wall was adobe capped with tile to throw off the rain. During this year the Church was adorned with six large oil paintings, one in each chapel.

At the end of this year the Indians existing at this Mission were 796.

A granary 45x6½ varas was built in 1799, plastered in and outside and tile roof. This was all the building done this year. Thirty-two new houses were erected in 1800 to accommodate that number of families, making with those erected in '98. in all fifty-one. These houses are being built to form streets, crossing at right angles, when the required number shall have been erected. Corridors were built inside the courtyard, on three sides of the Mission square, flooring and pillars of brick and mortar, roof of tile.

Number of Indians actually in the Mission, 864.

Thirty-one houses for the same number of families were built in 1801, equal in every respect to the fifty-one already reported. Another house 21x6 varas was built, divided into bedroom, hall, and kitchen; a corridor was built with it. This house for the use of head gardener and family.

Number actually existing in Mission, 1022.

Thirty-one houses were built in 1802, for that number of families, similar to the 82 built during the preceding years, making a total of 113 houses. A wall three varas high has been made on three sides of this square, leaving plenty of space for the houses yet to be erected. A house of adobe 20x6

varas, and three tanks of brick and mortar, were
built for a tannery. Adjoining the tannery, a
house was built for the Majordomo 18x6 varas,
with corridor, kitchen, hall, and bedrooms. Moreover, five other rooms were erected, for various
uses, in the Mission, the whole length 40x6 varas.
This year Dec. 31st, a tabular statement of all the
Missions was made by the President, Fr. Lasuen,
from the time of each foundation to date. when he
gave up charge.   .

Statement both spiritual and temporal of the
Mission of Santa Barbara, from its founding Dec.
4th, 1786, to Dec. 31st, 1802:

No. Baptisms.	No. Marriages.	Deaths.	Existing.
2.251	494	· 989	1,093

Cattle incl. 83 vk. Oxen.	No. Head Sheep.	No. of Mares and Foals.	No. of Tame Horses.	No. of Mules Tame.
2,100	9,082	427	215	58

	Wheat.	Barley.	Corn.	Beans.	Spanish Peas.	
For this y'r	113 ctls.	2 ctls.	90 ℔s.	9 ctls.	25 ℔s.	Sowed.
This Year's.	2876 ctls	40 ctls.	40 ctls.	000	10 ctls.	Har-vest.

Forty-eight new houses were erected in 1803,
for same number of families, making in all 161.
In order to attend better to the necessities of the
Indians, and facilitate their attendance at Mass

and instructions, a station was selected and a Church built on a large rancheria called "Sagshpileel," ever after called San Miguel, under whose patronage the Church was dedicated, about two leagues west of this Mission, near a laguna (the ruins of this chapel may yet be seen near the old house of Daniel Hill, at the "Patera"). The dimensions of this Church, 22x9, including walls.

Number of Indians existing at the end of this year, 1,792.

Thirty-seven new houses were erected in 1804, to accommodate that number of families. A mud wall was also built making a large yard for the use of the Indians. The number of Indians existing at the end of this year were 1783. The reason for the decrease in the number, was the founding on Sept. 17, of the Mission of Santa Ynez, which was nearer to the rancherias of several families baptized from Santa Barbara, who were enrolled in that Mission after above date; the number thus enrolled in Santa Ynez was 112 persons, 27 families, who otherwise would have been counted with the above.

This year a new corral was made at Tecolote, on the 28th, 29th and 30th of July, 1084 head of sheep were marked and exchanged at the Mission of San Buenaventura, for another band of same number, this band was sent to stock Tecolote. San Miguel ranch had 2710 head sheep, Cañada de las Armas 2280. and 2520 head black cattle divided among these places. The Mission owned this year 11.500 head sheep and 8500 head black cattle, mares and foals 540. tame horses 238 head. The ranch of "Mistwaghehewang." or San Marcos. was stocked this year from the above, besides a large vineyard was planted. and several houses built. one for Majordomo. the others for various uses of the ranch. and particularly as store rooms for vineyard. (The ruins of these houses can yet be seen on the ranch.)

All the ranchos east of Santa Ynez river, including San Marcos. belonged to the Mission of Santa Barbara, and the property extended to the "Rincon." All, or nearly all had now been stocked with various kinds of animals, such as black cattle, horses, sheep, goats, etc., and the best of the arable land was sown to wheat, corn, barley and various kinds of beans, peas, etc. The principal ranchos, for wheat and corn, were:

San Pedro y San Pablo or Dos Pueblos, called by the Indians "Mekeguwe."

San Estevan. in the native tongue, "Tokeene." and San Miguel. in the native tongue "Sagspileel" or "Mescaltitan."

Corn, beans, etc., were sown also in San Jose or Abajo, in San Juan Bautista or the Sauzal, this is at present a part of the Hope ranch, its location is east of and bordering on the Arroyo del Burro, the Modoc road absorbs a part of it nd runs through it as far as the bridge.

Tokeene or San Estevan is all that land north of the present stage road, beginning west of the Arroyo "Pedragoso" at the new bridge, and continuing to the Arroyo del Burro This plain was very fertile. The foundation of a large stone wall may yet be seen a little beyond the bridge west of Pedragoso. This was a large corral for various purposes, principally for tame horses. A spring of splendid water flows near Mr. Dixie Thompson's house.

Thirty-six houses, for that number of families, were built in 1805. Two large granaries and a house of the same size as granaries for lumber. The entire number of family houses for Indians was now 234.

A reservoir of stone and mortar was built in 1806, to collect water for the gardens, orchard, etc. Dimensions 40 varas square by $2\frac{1}{2}$ varas deep. This reservoir exists in a perfect state and is used by the water company to collect water to supply the City of Santa Barbara.

In 1807 a very strong dam was built across the "Pedragoso" creek, about a mile and one-half from the Mission, at a point high enough to allow water to flow in an open aqueduct into the mill reservoir. This mill and reservoir were built at the same time, behind the one used at present by the City Water Co. The mill is in ruins, and a small part of its reservoir near the hill has fallen in, but could be of service with a little repairing. The Indian village was enlarged this year by 18 more houses for families, total 252. Four more houses were erected for the soldiers, in front of the Church, distant in a straight line 150 varas.

In 1808 buildings were erected for manufacturing and baking pottery, water pipes, etc. An ornamental stone fountain and lavatory were built in front of the Mission. In 1809 the Priests' dwelling facing the Presidio, was enlarged by erecting another building of stone and mortar in front, with flat polished concrete roof. This work was continued through 1810 to 1811, when the new house was finished off with a heavy stone arched corridor, after which work commenced on the frontispiece of the Church, intending to improve and embellish it as much as possible, concerning which an account will be given when finished. (There was never any account given, as this Church building had to be taken down a few years after.) On the 21st, 22d, and several days after, of December, 1812, several severe earthquake shocks were felt; these shocks were so severe, that all the Mission buildings were badly injured, the Church in particular was so badly damaged that it was judged more expedient to take it down and build a new one, than to repair it.

The years 1813–14 were spent in repairing some of the buildings and taking down the old Church. The new stone Church was commenced in 1815, the work was pushed rapidly while the Mission buildings were being repaired at the same time. In 1817 the flat roof was removed from the principal house of the Mission, all the wood work completely renovated, then covered with a tiled gable roof.

The dimensions of the new Church are: Length, including walls, 60 varas; width, including walls, 14 varas; from floor to ceiling, 10 varas. Work was carried on during the years 1818 and 19 with such effect that on the tenth day of Sept., 1820, the Church was finished and blessed. The walls are of large cubes of cut sandstone, and nearly six feet through, nevertheless they were further strengthened by heavy solid stone buttresses at each angle, and at sections along the sides. Without doubt it is the strongest Mission Church building in California. One tower of two stories held six bells, three of which were stationary, the others with yoke. In a niche in the frontispiece, supported by six columns, is a statue of our Patroness Santa Barbara, cut from the best stone found here and painted. The apex and angles of the frontispiece are adorned with stone statues, representing respectively the three theological virtues, Faith, Hope and Charity. The interior is neatly finished.

the walls all plastered, the columns and cornice
frescoed, the ceiling lathed, hard finished, and
ornamented with designs from Vitruvius, cut from
cedar and painted. The floor of red cement made
from oil and lime, is hard and finely polished.
The altars are neatly ornamented with fine cruci-
fixes and statues in wood. Over the high altar
on a bracket in the wall, stands a statue in wood
of Santa Barbara; on each side of Santa Barbara
is a painting on the canvas wall piece of St.
Joachim and St. Ann. Directly under these are
the statues in wood of the Blessed Virgin and St.
Joseph on brackets. Small wooden statues of St.
Dominic and St. Francis, may be seen, one on
each side of the high altar on pillars. The walls
of the sanctuary are adorned, one side with a painting of the "Infierno" and Day of Judgment, a poor
copy of Murillo in the "Escorial" in Spain.
Facing this is a good painting of Our Lady of the
Scapular. Outside the sanctuary, on the wall,
hangs a large painting of the Assumption and
Coronation of the Blessed Virgin, and facing it
one of the same size of the Crucifixion. All the
above works of art were brought from Mexico for
this Mission in 1798, together with the fourteen
stations which are hung along the walls at equal
distances. During the last twenty years the
Church has been adorned with several paintings,
St. Francis Solano, called the Apostle of Peru, on

a column; over a side altar hangs one of the
Blessed Virgin of the seven Dolors; below this is
a good one of Our Lady of Guadalupe; in front of
this is a very good picture of St. Joseph and the
Child Jesus; in the small chapels can be seen St.
Anthony of Padua and St. Catherine of Alexan-
dria. Over the door of the Sacristy hangs a
splendid copy of Rubens' Descent from the Cross.
Inside the Sacristy, over the vestment drawers,
can be seen a splendid painting, which represents.
according to St. Anselm, the dress worn by Our
Lord and Savior, as painted by St. Luke; another
represents the baptism of Our Lord by St. John.
The Ambulatory is hung with several old and very
good paintings; on one canvas are seen the three
Archangels, St. Michael, St. Gabriel and St.
Raphael, on another of the same size are St. Clare,
St. Rose and St. Agnes. Three represent respect-
ively, St. Francis of Assisi, St. Bonaventure and
St. Peter Nolascus. and one beautiful painting of
our Lady, under the appellation of Refuge of
Sinners.

CHAPTER VII.

Had I not promised information down to the
present day, my work should have finished with
the preceding chapter; because, the principal

buildings being repaired, and this Church finished, dedicated and blessed, the Mission was considered complete; so much so, that. excepting the Indian family houses. no other buildings of any importance were erected after this.

The District Governors, even under the rule of Spain, taxed the Missions to support what they called the government of the King, and often imposed *excessive* contributions, even to the detriment of the Indians of the Missions. Santa Barbara suffered in this respect in proportion to the others, if not more. In those days money was very scarce, and cattle, sheep, wool, etc., very low in price, so to meet any heavy "contribution," so called, a large number of cattle, etc., should be disposed of in some way. Extra demands were made amounting to' as much as four thousand dollars; these demands were considered very unjust, being made without authority of the King. Still, all this was very moderate compared with what the Missions had to suffer shortly after the independence of Mexico.

Information was received in 1833 that the Missions had been deprived of *all* their property; but the Congress of 1835 revoked the decree of spoliation, by another, restoring to the Church the property of which it had been deprived.

This district which comprised upper and lower California, or as it was called at that time both

Californias, "Ambas Californias," was under the spiritual jurisdiction of the Bishop of Sonora. In 1835 the same Congress that had restored the Church property, determined that the Californias should have a Bishop proper; who would naturally be more interested in the growth and advancement, both spiritual and temporal, of the country. In accordance with this resolution the Government decreed, and published on the 19th of Sept., 1836. "That one of the three persons named by the Metropolitan Chapter, should be selected and proposed to the Holy See, for Bishop of both Californias;" also that the Bishop elect should receive from the public Treasury, the sum of six thousand dollars a year. until such time as the Diocese would have rents or income sufficient for the support becoming his dignity; also, that for the journey to his Diocese and other immediate necessary expenses, he should receive three thousand dollars, and finally, that all the property pertaining to the Pious Fund of California should be placed at the disposal of him and his successors, to be by them administered, according to the will of its founders·

The desired object was not obtained until 1840, when Fr. Francisco Garcia Diego y Moreno was elected first Bishop of California by Pope Gregory XVI. and consecrated with august solemnity by three Bishops. in the Church of his College of Our Lady of Guadalupe Zacatecas, on the 4th of October.

Shortly after, he issued his first Pastoral to the clergy and laity of his Diocese. He arrived in California December, 1841, landing at San Diego; and at Santa Barbara on the 11th of January. 1842, when he took formal possession of the Diocese amidst the greatest rejoicing. This Mission was selected as his ordinary residence, and Santa Barbara was looked upon as the Episcopal City. He died at the Mission April 30, 1846. A tablet over his tomb at the right, or epistle side, of the high altar, bears the following inscription:

Hic jacet ill^{mus}, ac Rev^{mus}, D. D. Fr.
Fran. Garcia Diego et Moreno,
Primus Ep^{us} hujus Diœcesis
Californ. Qui pridie Kalendas
Maii, Anni Domini MDCCCXLVI. ex
hac vita Migravit.

It may not be out of place to state here that the Missions of California were offered to the College of Our Lady of Guadalupe in 1832, to divide the work with San Fernando, and replace those who had acquired a right to leave. The College accepted the charge, and elected Fr. Garcia Diego Commissary Prefect, who came to California and received the Missions in 1833 from Fr. Duran. Fr. Gonzales Rubio received the Mission of San Jose at that time and made an inventory and report of that Mission up to 1840. In the following list are the names of those who came from the College of Guadalupe, between 1833 and '42.

Fr. Garcia Diego, afterwards Bishop in '40.

Fr. Bernardino Perez.

Fr. Rafael Moreno.

Fr. J. N. Anzar.

Fr. Jose M. Gutierrez.

Fr. Juan Mercado.

Fr. Jose M. Gonzalez Rubio.

Fr. Lorenzo Quijas.

Fr. Antonio Real.

Fr. Jose M. Real.

Fr. Miguel Muro.

Fr. Franciso de J. Sanchez.

Fr. Trinidad Macias.

Fr. Marcelo Velasco.

Fr. N. Pedrosa.

Fr. N. Acosta.

Frs. Francisco and Jose Flores also came, but only as visitors.

Santa Barbara is the only Mission in California of which may be truly said. it was never without a Franciscan, from its founding to the present day. Below are the names of the *principal* Ministers from 1786 to 1836.

Fr. Antonio Paterna, founder and first Minister.

Fr. Christobal Oramas.

Fr. Jose de Miguel.

Fr. Estevan Tapis.

Fr. Juan Cortes.

Fr. Marcos Amestoy.

Fr. Marcos Vtoria.

Fr. Luis Gilde Taboada.

Fr. Ramon Olbis.

Fr. Antonio Ripoll.

Fr. Francisco Suñer.

Fr. Antonio Jayme.

Fr. Juan Moreno.

Fr. Antonio Jimeno, who signed the report of 1836, which was the last rendered to the *Government* of Mexico concerning this Mission and copied in the register. The Ministers, however, continued to report the state of the Missions to their Prefects, up to the arrival of the Bishop. These reports were ordinarily made in letter form and sent by the Prefects to the Colleges of San Fernando and Guadalupe. In proof of this I have a part of the original document from which Father Gonzales Rubio made his report of the Mission of San Jose up to the year 1841. After the arrival of the Bishop a report should be made to him also. consequently we see that what Bancroft asserts, viz.: "After 1836 no further reports were made" is not quite correct. Mr. Bancroft also states, that after this year "the *Community*" was broken up, and it appears he refers particularly to Santa Barbara. I do not pretend to know what *Mr. Bancroft* means by the "Community," but I do know that more Franciscan Priests resided together at this Mission from 1836 to 1845, and after than ever before. Fr. Antonio Jimeno continued here in company with Fr. Jose Jimeno, his brother, and Fr. Duran, Fr. Gonzales resided here in 1842, the Bishop, Fr. Sanchez, etc., yet what *we* understand by a "*Community*" strictly did not exist in any Mission, even from their commencement. The reports above referred to and many other valuable documents sent to San Fernando for safety, were preserved with all possible care. In 1860, as soon as the expulsion of the Religious Orders became general, all these documents relating to California and its Missions, together with a vast number of priceless historical MSS., and other valuable papers were boxed up and taken to the private dwelling of the Syndic of San Fernando for safe keeping. Such was the demoniacal hatred excited against the Religion, however, that nothing they possessed was safe. Even these documents and MSS., that one would imagine the Government would use all its endeavors to preserve, when found by *officers* of the *Government* were taken by their orders from the private house of the Syndic and burned publicly on the streets of the City of Mexico. This information I have on the testimony of an eye witness, Very Rev. Fr. Isidore Camacho, present Guardian of San Fernando.

Moreover, during the chaos and confusion of

Alvarado's rule. from 1836 to 1842, and the war between the United States and Mexico. it seemed that soldiers arrogated to themselves an unbridled license, to do and act as they pleased. Many Missions were completely gutted. no regard was had for books, papers, reports, MSS., or documents of any kind. Instances are reported where valuable documents and MSS., were used for gun wads and cigarette paper. In viewing these facts it is surprising, but Providential, that even the few documents we have at the present day, should have been saved from the general ruin.

In April 1845, the Congress of Mexico decreed that all the unsold property of the Pious Fund, quasi confiscated in 1842, should be restored to the administration of Bishop Garcia Diego, who had gone there to protest against its confiscation and having obtained the above decree returned to Santa Barbara the same year.

The following facts cannot fail to interest persons doing business in this county, as it shows the great difference in the value of property and real estate between that time and now.

In 1845 Father Duran prepared to leave and was very anxious to resign the administration of all the property of this Mission. He wrote to Pico and was told he could deliver the administration to any person in whom he had sufficient confidence, or lease the property for the benefit of the

Bishop, Ministers and Indians. Consequently in July, 1845, an inventory was taken and the property of the Mission appraised by J. Manso, Andres Pico and Fr. Duran. Having reserved this church and the principal house for the use of the Bishop and Priests the remainder was appraised as follows:

Valuation of Santa Barbara Mission property:

Thirty-three rooms	$1,500
Store house and goods	1,552
Cellars and contents	768
Soap factory, etc	398
Tannery, etc	250
Blacksmith shop, tools, etc	160
Weavers' rooms, looms, etc	126
Carpenters' shop, etc	34
Majordomo's house	385
Saddles and vaquero's outfit	24
Orchard of 512 fruit trees	1,500
Two vineyards, one with 1,295 vines, the other 2,400 vines	1,720
Cattle, 816 head; horses, 398 head; mules, 9 head	3,545
Corrals	265
San Jose Vineyard, containing 2,262 vines and 100 trees	1,335
Cieneguita with crops	300
San Antonio (a corral at Cieneguita)	25

Rancho of San Marcos, with vineyard,

buildings, grain and live stock on it, viz:
cattle, 140 head; horses, 90 head; sheep,
1,730 head........ 6,956

All the above property was leased in December,
1845, to N. A. Den and Daniel Hill, at a yearly
rental of $1,200, for the benefit as already stated.
In the lease it was stipulated that the Indians
should be entirely free to work for the lessees, or
for themselves.

At the death of Bishop Garcia Diego, Very Rev.
Fr. Jose M. Gonzalez Rubio became Administrator
of the whole Diocese. His administration was
noted for singular ability, prudence, and foresight.
As the Diocese was very large and clergy few, Fr.
Langlois received from him in 1849 faculties of
Vicar for the northern part, with instructions to
purchase some pieces of land for ecclesiastical purposes in San Francisco, before it should become
too valuable by the great influx of population.
The property on which St. Francis church now
stands was purchased at that time.

In the latter part of 1850, Fr. Gonzalez surren-
dered his administration to the Rt. Rev. J. S.
Alemany, who had been consecrated in June of
the same year at Rome, Bishop of Monterey, but
at the earnest request of the Bishop he retained
the office of Vicar General.

In February, 1852, a petition, to establish a
Franciscan Convent or College, with a Novitiate

for the education of young men in the Sacred Ministry for California, was sent to Rome, and granted.

Bishop Alemany by his letter of Jan. 6th, 1853, assigned this Mission for the objects stated in the petition, and stated, in case this Mission should not be adapted for a College or Convent he would assign another place in his Diocese.

A meeting of the Franciscan Fathers was held Jan. 7, 1853. Present: Bishop Alemany, Fr. J. M. Gonzalez, V. G., J. J. Orruño, Guardian of San Fernando, Jose Jimeno, Prefect of Missions, Fr. Antonio Jimeno, Fr. Francisco Sanchez, and by unanimous consent this Mission was considered erected into a Hospice, as the beginning of what was to be an Apostolic College of Propaganda Fidei, and Fr. Jose Jimeno, of the College of San Fernando, was the first President.

Fr. Jose Jimeno did not consider these buildings fit for a College of Propaganda, he therefore selected a place in the City of Santa Barbara, the Bishop approving, and purchased the site of the present new parish church and residence. The church was commenced immediately, the house fitted up for occupation and on Sunday, July 23, 1854. it was solemnly declared, and announced in the presence of a very large congregation, that the Apostolic College, the titular of which was the Blessed Virgin of the Seven Dolors, was then and there founded and established. The novitiate was then opened by giving the Habit to five novices, viz.: Jose Godayol, Francisco Codina, Jose Alcina, Geronimo Lopez and Jose Hermeneguildo, these two lay brothers.

Bishop Alemany was elected or appointed Archbishop of San Francisco, and took possession of that See, July 29, 1853. His successor in the Diocese of Monterey was Rt. Rev. Thaddeus Amat, a man eminently versed in the science of Theology and ecclesiastical lore, who had been called by the Bishop of Philadelphia as his Theologian to the Seventh Provincial Council of Baltimore held in 1849. Arriving at Santa Barbara the Bishop preferred to have the Parish Church and residence in the City, rather than at the Mission, where it was at that time, He concluded arrangements with the Franciscan Fathers in Santa Barbara, and having obtained the approbation of the authorities at Rome by letters dated July 6, 1856, the transfer and exchange so much desired by the Rt. Rev. Bishop was effected the same year. By this change the Franciscan Fathers, received the perpetual use of these Mission buildings, Church, two orchards and vineyard, while their church and residence in the City of Santa Barbara passed into and became property of the Diocese.

Before the above said transfer took place the President of the College, Fr. Jose Jimeno, died.

His brother Fr. Antonio Jimeno succeeded him, pro tempore, in virtue of the Constitutions of the Order.

In 1859, Very Rev. Fr. Gonzalez Rubio was appointed President of the College, and in consequence resigned the office of Vicar General, which he had held up to that time under each Bishop of the Diocese. During his term of President of the College, seven young men were ordained Priests, viz.: In Aug., 1860, Jose Godayol, Fr. Francisco Codina and Jose Alcina; in Dec, 1864, Fr. B. Sheehan and B. Fox; in Sept., 1868, Fr. J. J. O'Keefe and Fr. P. Wade. Father Gonzalez became very much discouraged at the turn things had taken, so different from what he could have reasonably expected. His health began to fail, on which account he wrote several times to the General of the Order asking to be relieved of his responsibility as President. His petition was not granted until 1871, when Very Rev. J. M. Romo, who six years before had been commissioned by the ill-fated Maximilian to establish a Franciscan hospice for Mexicans in the Holy Land, which was never effected owing to the Emperor's death, was sent by the General to relieve Father Gonzalez.

Father Romo arrived in California, January, 1872, received letters patent from the General in May, by virtue of which, he became Guardian of

the College, and took formal possession of the
office in June.

Perceiving that this College was too far removed
from other houses of the Order and that in a com-
paratively new country like California, there
would necessarily be a lack of vocations to the
Sacred Ministry, he resolved to visit his native
country Mexico, believing he could obtain a number of Priests and novices there, to increase the
working staff of this house. With the General's
permission he started on his journey in May, 1879,
and after a lapse of three years he returned in
1882, undeceived, and somewhat discouraged at
his failure.

Under these circumstances, having consulted
with a member of the house, he reported minutely
to the General all he had endeavored to accom-
plish, showing the difficulties under which this
house labored and giving as his opinion that it
could not progress, isolated as it was and independent of every other house and province of the
Order; praying at the same time that it might be
annexed to some province in the East, firmly
established, and from which it would receive the
aid and assistance of additional members. The
General on receiving the reports stated, judged it
more prudent before deciding, to delegate a member of the Order, to make an official visitation and
final report.

The visitation was made in August, 1884, by Very Rev. Ferdinand Bergmeyer, whose report being made, the following decree was issued in conformity with the desire of all concerned.

DECREE.

As the most Rev. Minister General of the Regular Observance of the Order of St. Francis, has earnestly requested that the College of Our Lady of Seven Dolors of Santa Barbara, in the Diocese of Monterey and Los Angeles, both for the greater increase of the same College and for the greater extension of the Order of St. Francis in California, be changed (from its independent state) and annexed to the Province of the Sacred Heart of Jesus of the United States of North America. His Holiness Pope Leo XIII, in an audience on the 19th of April, 1885, having heard the report of Archbishop Jacobini, Secretary of Propaganda, kindly consented that the aforesaid College should be incorporated with the Province of the most Sacred Heart of Jesus.

Given at Rome from the Chambers of the Sacred Congregation of Propaganda Fidei, May 5th, 1885.

JOANES CARD. SIMEONI,
Prefectus.

† D. ARCHIEP. TYRENSIS,
Secret.

The above decree was executed as soon as possible. On July 15th, Very Rev. Fr. Ferdinand Bergmeyer, O. S. F., was elected in Provincial Chapter, Guardian of this College, and received commission and letters patent dated Aug. 6th, 1885, to take formal possession of said College with all and everything belonging to it, in the name of the Province, which has been done to the great benefit of this College, which now forms an integral part of the Province of the Sacred Heart of Jesus. The Provincial house is in the City of St. Louis, Mo. As it seems incumbent on me to say a few words regarding the aforesaid Province, to which this Mission and College now belong, I will state for the information of the public in general that this Province of the Sacred Heart was established in the United States by Franciscan Priests who came here on a Mission in 1858, from the old Province of the Holy Cross in Saxony, established in 1223; three years before the death of St. Francis, Founder of the Order. In 1879 being well provided with Priests, lay Brothers, Scolastics, houses for studies, etc., it separated from the old Province, and is now on a firm basis; having the novitiate, and house for the study of humanities, at Teutopolis, Ill.; higher studies including Mental Philosophy, at St. Francis College, Quincy, Ill., and Theology at St. Louis, Mo.

It numbers, houses, 26; Priests, 130; Scolastics, 50: Lay Brothers, 200, nearly all these skilled in some branch of mechanical art. Any of the above members may be sent on Missions or to supply any house of the Province, as necessity may require.

FINIS.

EXPLANATORY NOTES.

It must not be supposed that the Churches enumerated in the preceding pages, exist at present. The gradual and continued increase of the baptized Indians made it necessary either to enlarge the church or build a new one, the latter was preferred, and the serviceable material of the former was used in constructing the latter.

The Indians commenced the day with morning prayer, then a part of the catechism, after the work. In the evening short catechetical instructions and prayer; on Sundays and Holy days of obligation, after the ordinary devotions, they received a more thorough explanation of the Christian doctrine.

The most intelligent were taught reading, writing, and to sing by note, also arithmetic, while many showed a partiality for the various mechanical arts, and even a talent for sculpture, all which was encouraged by the fathers.

All the Indians of Santa Barbara Channel spoke the same language and learned Spanish very easily.

The secularization of the Missions, the confiscation and spoliation of their property by the Mexican government or its agents, and the leasing or renting of what little remained to parties who generally seldom or ever paid the Indians the part to which they were entitled, are the principal causes of the dispersion of the Mission Indians of California.

9 783337 039134